C000183379

Legend

ISBN: 978-1-952840-10-4

UNITED HOUSE Publishing
Waterford, Michigan
info@unitedhousepublishing.com
www.unitedhousepublishing.com

Cover by Pillmore Designs.

Printed in the United States of America

To Mary Cox Clardy, my mother, devoted to me for 61 wonderful years, with love.

Stacy Clardy, 1958, in photo taken by his wife Peggy

TABLE OF CONTENTS

ABOUT THE AUTHOR

After seeing the world, Stacy Clardy now resides on the creek at the south end of Pawleys Island, South Carolina. He is a retired naval captain. He enjoys his daily jog, fishing, waterskiing and a good game of golf. He has been a real estate agent since his retirement in 1982. This is his first book.

CHAPTER ONE
Columbia, South Carolina
1936-1945

All Glory and Praise to God! The Lord decided through his grace that I, Stacy Clardy, should be born on February 17, 1936, weighing in at seven pounds and thirteen ounces at 12:25pm on a Monday afternoon at the Columbia Hospital.

I was a healthy baby only having one abnormality! My tongue was tied and soon after that my parents found out about it and had my tongue "clipped." Later on, some of my best friends and teachers wished they had left it unclipped. Mother also taped my ears back because she wanted a perfect looking son, not one favoring Mickey Mouse.

My father, Herman Stacy Clardy, was a graduate of the University of Virginia Law School in the class of 1931. My mother, Mary Cox Clardy, was a graduate of the School of Nursing at the same university, and that is where they met. My father's family

Herman Stacy Clardy, Citadel, 1927-8

Henry and Bertie Clardy, Wedding Day, 1906

consisted of his mother, Bertie, better known to me as NaNa, and a sister, Bertie Maude Clardy, and her husband Mark Sylvester. They resided in Columbia in an apartment near Five Points.

7

Cox Family, 1910, Stacy's Mother is second from right

My mother's family consisted of five brothers and three sisters. They resided in Charlottesville, Virginia. Her brothers were Charles Edward, Ellis, Rossa, Lynn and Roy. She had three sisters and they were Lucy, Alva and Daisy.

My father was employed by the Federal Land Bank in Columbia as a lawyer, and my mother was a housewife. We lived at the time of my birth about one block up Devine Street from the Five Points area. During this period of time in Columbia, we also lived on South Saluda and Cline Street which was north of Dreher High School.

My early schooling included Vacation Bible School. I remember as a little guy, maybe 4 years old, being required to stand up before all of the parents and recite verses. That was my first public speaking engagement in my career. As a first grader, I attended Schneider Elementary on Devine Street. We were living about four blocks from

Stacy, 1942, Columbia

8

the school on Cline Street, and I walked to school with some of the children in the neighborhood. My first grade teacher was Miss Smith. My second grade teacher was Miss Henderson, and my third grade teacher was Miss Van Landingham.

My early interests were basically in sports. We played kickball, rode bicycles and had a big old time in Columbia. My only sibling, a sister named Mary Susan, was born on October 13, 1940 at the Providence Hospital. I remember war bonds and neighbors who had been in the Pearl Harbor area during World War II.

Stacy and sister, Susan, 1943

I also remember making trips with my mother to Charlottesville, Virginia to visit her family. I recall that on one trip with two of her friends, the car in which we were riding hit some ice on the road and turned over several times. The impact broke a bone in my mother's shoulder because she was shielding me from harm as we rolled over. The other two people in the front seat were not hurt. We all walked away from the accident, but we had to cancel the trip and return home.

One of my memories is of a bull dog by the name of Spot. He stayed in our fenced backyard, which Spot did not like. He had a way of running into the fence with his backside eventually making a hole in the fence. We could not keep him inside the fence after this happened. My father eventually decided to give Spot to a farmer so he could run free.

There was a girl by the name of Ann Mickle and a boy by the name of Tommy Wilcox who both lived within a block of my house, and we all walked to school together. I have a memory of a girl named Patsy Cooper who lived in the apartment next door to NaNa, Bertie Maude and Mark. I remember her very well as one of my first best friends.

CHAPTER TWO
Andrews, South Carolina
1945-1951

The family moved to Andrews because my Daddy wanted to practice law in his home town. We moved into NaNa's home on North Morgan Avenue just across the street from the Andrews School System. The school consisted of three buildings and a gymnasium. I attended school in Andrews from the fourth grade through the ninth grade. My beloved teachers were Miss Lovell, Miss Kite, Miss Hyman, Miss Gibson, Miss Crosby and Mr. Woodberry who taught me the three R's: reading, 'riting and 'rithmetic!

There was an apartment on the side of NaNa's home. In 1949, NaNa, Bertie and her baby daughter Suzanna, moved into the apartment next to us. NaNa maintained a garden in the side yard where she grew beans, tomatoes, squash, watermelon, cantaloupe and potatoes. I helped her with the garden. She also had a chicken coop with three or four hens and a rooster. My job was to kill a chicken for her when she needed one to cook! I had a method that involved taking a broomstick and placing it over the chicken's neck, then pulling up on its legs and removing the chicken's head. I would put it in a pan so it wouldn't get dirty. My grandmother thought I was an excellent chicken killer!

My other important job was to bring in coal for NaNa's cooking stove. I also learned how to make slingshots and I became very efficient at shooting them! I used either marbles or a small stone to go bird hunting. I killed different types of edible birds, and my grandmother prepared them for me as a treat! We also used the slingshots for playing war games in the neighborhood.

There was not a lot to do in Andrews, so my friends and I would break up into two teams, declare war on each other and shoot china-berries in slingshots at one another in the countryside of Andrews. We had a great old time! Fortunately, during all this time we did not hurt anyone seriously. But if you got hit anywhere, it made a big whelp and hurt! These slingshot wars became a feature article in two of the local papers in Georgetown and Pawleys Island in later years, which appears at the end of this chapter.

I served on the school safety patrol during this time, and our job allowed us to be dismissed from classes early, so we could go stand on the corner near the school in order to help the first and second graders across the street. We took off early and sometimes went to the local pool room to shoot pool instead of going to the street corner to help the children cross the street. One day while we were in the pool hall in Ozburn's café on Main Street, we were leaning over the pool table, and Superintendent Mr. Garris came in the door, grabbed us and took us back to school. He called our parents, and my mother could not believe what we had done. We all were expelled for a day.

The principal, Mr. E. C. Rhodes, was a man who believed in punishment. He had a nice long paddle with a handle; if you misbehaved, you were sent to him for an office visit, and you knew what to expect. I think I suffered from some kind of attention deficit problem, because I often got in trouble. I talked too much or was reprimanded for some other failure to stay on task, so my teacher would send me down to the principal's office. A friend of mine by the name of Jackie Powers and I set a record in the seventh grade for getting the most "lickins" in one year. I think the number of times was a dozen.

My primary interests during this period of time were in sports. I did not weigh enough to make the varsity football team in the ninth grade. You had to weigh at least 100 pounds and I only weighed 92, so Coach Fleishman made me the team's manager. In the ninth grade, I did make the varsity basketball and baseball teams and lettered in each of those sports. I was a better basketball player than a baseball player.

Another activity that was very important to me at this time was the Boy Scouts. I joined the Scouts at age 11, so I had three years in the Scouts in Andrews before moving. I eventually became a Life Scout. We went to camp down near Charleston called Camp Ho Non Wah. It had a pool there, so I earned my swimming badge while at camp. This was the first time that I ever saw a swimming pool. I went to camp there for three years, and I participated in all of the sports. While there, I won several fifty-yard races along with other shorter distance races.

Boy Scouts was very interesting and a lot of fun for me. There was a terrific bunch of kids participating in the Boy Scouts along with me. Also, there was a great Scout Master by the name of Jerome Moskow.

Another activity I enjoyed as a child was going down to Black River. It was a beautiful river, and we would get someone to take us down to it; sometimes we even hiked down there. We swam in the river and dove out of the cypress trees amongst many alligators and water moccasins, and they did not seem to bother us. We really enjoyed ourselves there.

I also learned to play the alto saxophone and participated in the school band for one year. Then sports took over. You were not allowed to be in both the band and sports.

In the seventh or eighth grade, I became interested in girls. My first girlfriend was Peggy Bath, and she gave me my first kiss. Other girlfriends of mine during this time period in my life were: Vera Blakeley, Doris Norton, Patricia Hemingway and Joan Green. We attended parties and played Spin the Bottle, and when the bottle pointed to a girl, the boy had to kiss that girl. I remember a girl named Bronte Barrineau who could kiss better than anybody else, mostly because she used her tongue.

Every summer we spent two weeks at Pawleys Island. Daddy would rent a house: Usually it was the Carraway house. It had a separate outside kitchen and quarters for the maid, Minnie Shurbrick, who always went with us. It was beside the pier that exists today, which back in those days was public. I got up at first light and went down on the beach to catch fish like drum, whiting and spots. I caught fish almost every morning, and we ate the fish during the day. This was a great time in my life.

In 1951, I remember having a house party at a cottage called the Chapel View that was located across the street from the Pawleys Island Chapel and is still there today. It was a two-story apartment. While at the house party, my friend Billy Barrineau and I got in a scuffle by the outdoor shower that was located along the side of the house. He picked me up, we began to wrestle, and we fell over the rail from the second floor to the bottom floor. I fell on my back and broke my left arm and dislocated my wrist. He fell on his head, and it did not even hurt him.

Simmie Britt and Fernie Rhem had a car so they took me to the emergency room at the Georgetown Hospital. My mother showed up thirty minutes later. The doctors gave me ether to put me to sleep, so the doctor could set my arm. Unfortunately, I had eaten a lot of lime sherbet ice cream so when I woke up from the anesthesia, the whole room was covered in the lime sherbet that I had regurgitated. To this day, I dislike lime sherbet.

I had a Collie by the name of King. He liked to attend church where we were members at Trinity Methodist, which was about four blocks from our home. King proceeded before us each Sunday and lay on the front steps of the church waiting for our family to arrive. He liked to see the people who were coming into the church!

Suzanna Sylvester and Stacy with King on So. Morgan Avenue, across the street from Andrews School in Andrews, 1946

As a child, I suffered from allergies. My mother had me tested by a dermatologist, who found that I was allergic to everything. I took shots once a week for my allergies. Later in the eighth grade, I began having asthma attacks once a year around Thanksgiving and Christmas. My mother insisted that I take cod liver oil and made me take naps. I guess it worked because I outgrew the asthma.

On one of our trips to Black River, a friend of mine by the name of Buck Burns went with us. A few days later

Buck came down with polio. My mother heard about Buck getting polio, so she marched down to the local theater where I was watching a Saturday matinee, snatched me up to my surprise, took me home and put me in the bed! She made me rest and rest, worrying about me. Fortunately, no one else who was with us came down with polio. Buck Burns became paralyzed from the waist down as a result of that disease.

Below is an article written years later in *The Georgetown Times* about the property in Andrews where I hung out with some of my friends as a young boy, playing war games with our homemade sling shots and shooting china-berries with them against each other! It was written by a journalist for the *Times*, Tim Callahan, in March of 2009:

Pawleys Island resident Stacy Clardy thinks it's time Andrews got some good news in the paper.

Thanks to volunteers, and contributors like Clardy, who lived in Andrews as a child, Habitat for Humanity is providing that good news.

The fourth home to be built in Andrews on property Clardy donated on South Rosemary Avenue is not too far from becoming a reality. The property used to be used for "war games" by young local men in the 1940's and 50's.

"The prospective home-owner is nearing the end of her 400 hours of sweat equity working on other homes," said Annette Perreau, executive director of Habitat Georgetown County. Once that is complete, work on her home can begin. She has to purchase the home with a $1,000 down payment. Her monthly, no-interest mortgage payments will average around $320.

The third home on the property at 411 South Rosemary Avenue was dedicated in the fall to Bozie Mercer, a former Andrews High School student and long-time Habitat volunteer and employee.

Clardy and Mercer attended the high school at the same time. However, Clardy's family moved to Georgetown after his freshman year for the black and gold in 1951.

Back from 1947-1950, Clardy said some 11 to 14 year olds used the property for "war games" utilizing sling shots and china berries.

"There were no televisions or cell phones to entertain back then," he said.

Many of the participants' names locals will recognize: Clardy, Bozie, Bubby Mercer, Billy McDaniel, Phifer Payne, Walter Payne, Billy Barrineau, Johnny Pitts, Reid Saxon, Lloyd Morris, Royce Green and William Green.

The boys chose sides and went to war.

"Fortunately no one was seriously hurt during the games," said Clardy, who later really went to war as a Captain of a destroyer ship.

CHAPTER THREE
Georgetown, South Carolina
1951-1954

Clardy Family Christmas, 1953

The family moved to Georgetown after Daddy was elected the County Probate Judge in a race against Clayman Grimes. The position accorded him an office in the court house, where he presided over state matters and family court issues. He also practiced civil and criminal law. We moved into a duplex at 314 Orange Street near Duncan Methodist Church, where we became members. My mother went back to her profession of nursing where she joined the staff at Georgetown Memorial Hospital. Susan went to Winyah High School. She was four grades behind me.

I attended Winyah High School from the tenth through twelfth grades. This school was about four times the size of Andrews, and I did not adjust well to the larger school environment. I managed to pass the tenth grade but did not play sports. I joined

Winyah High Basketball Team with Coach Dufford

the Boy Scouts, but the troop was not run well, so I quit. I did learn to play golf at the Georgetown Country Club, where I won the First Flight Championship in 1953. I adjusted finally in the eleventh grade and made the varsity basketball and golf teams.

My best friend was Deal Smith. We hunted ducks on the Black River, doves and quail at Sampit and enjoyed deer drives at Santee. I joined the U.S. Naval Reserve in 1953 as a seaman recruit and attended Boot Camp in Bainbridge, Maryland during the summer with my friend Salters McClary. Other friends were Chip Hines, Bobby Ford, George O'Hara and Gerald Carter who joined me on the golf team.

In the twelfth grade, I made first string on the basketball team and was selected as one of the captains. I played guard alongside Bobby Rowe, forwards Deal Smith and Larry Joe Bass and center Wesley Wicker. That year, the team's record was 19-4 and was runner-up in the lower state's championship tournament in Or-

Basketball Champions, 1954

angeburg, South Carolina. This 1954 record lasted until 1985. The team also won the first beach ball classic at Myrtle Beach, defeating Mullins and Conway for the championship.

I also dated: Ginger Hinson (with whom I went to the Kingstree Junior-Senior Cotillion), Laura Jones, Doris Kelly and Peggy Boyle. Other girlfriends were: Beverly

Stacy and Ginger Hinson, 1953

Parlor, Alice Cox, Betty Whittle and Betty Ann Holliday. I was selected by my peers as Best Dancer, a senior superlative, with Carol Jean Carter.

To keep up with all my dating expenses, I bagged groceries at the A&P food store for $0.90 an hour. I also worked in the meat department cutting up chickens, and I was placed in charge of the produce department when the manager was not there. The manager, Mr. Palmer, had a girlfriend who was one of the cashiers in the store. She liked the way I bagged groceries so she made me stay in her "stall" for hours. This got old quickly, so I quit. I also found work at the movie theater as a ticket taker, but my commitment to the golf team interfered, so I had to leave that job, too. Also, I maintained the yard at home for some extra dollars.

Stacy and Peggy Boyle, Senior Prom, 1954

I spent my summers going to the Pawleys Island pavilion and shagging to the music of the old juke box. Shirlie Calhoun was one of the outstanding shaggers there who taught me moves that I still do today. Dale Cromartie, Deal Smith and I bought a pair of fiberglass water skis and went skiing many times behind Mr. Smith's 14-foot plywood boat that was powered by a ten-horsepower mercury motor in the creek at Pawleys Island and in Black River at Browns Ferry. I graduated from high school in May of 1954 and was accepted into the fresh-man class that fall at the University of South Carolina (USC) and the Naval ROTC program.

U. S. NAVAL TRAINING CENTER
RECRUIT TRAINING COMMAND
BAINBRIDGE, MD.
COMPANY 21 R

Boot Camp, 1953

Washington, D.C., Senior Trip, 1954

CHAPTER FOUR
Columbia, South Carolina
1954-1958

Midshipman Ball NROTC at USC, 1956

I attended the University of South Carolina for a one-week summer camp and lived in a cabin with three other freshmen. Sumner Waite was our senior advisor during the week. I registered to major in Economics in the Business School and in Naval Science.

My freshman year, I resided in a three bedroom apartment building on campus near the Russell House. My roommates were Salters McClary, Allen Johnson and Brock Conrad. I pledged the Phi Kappa Sigma fraternity in my sophomore year, moving into the fraternity house for the last three years of college. My roommates were Michael Cory for two years and Hamilton Dix for the last year. My future wife, Peggy Boyle, was chosen "Phi Kappa Sigma Girl" during our senior year. She attended Columbia College her freshman year. Peggy roomed with Judy Ward, a classmate of ours at Winyah High. She then transferred to USC.

I worked one summer at the Esso station on the corner of Front and Fraser Street in Georgetown for Fletcher Carter, a friend of mine who played on the same basketball team at Winyah High School. I played intramural sports at USC in football and golf. Roger Groves and I won the fraternity championship in golf for two straight years. I became engaged to Peggy Boyle my senior year.

As a ROTC midshipman, we were required to finish in four years. This meant that I had to take six courses each semester for four years and attend class six days a week. I was able to finish in four years by attending two summer schools. My grades were average, and I finished in the bottom half of my graduating class.

The guest speaker for our graduation ceremony was the senator from Massachusetts, John Fitzgerald Kennedy, who later became President of the United States of America in 1960. My father had a little reception at the Columbia Hotel after my graduation, and one of the guests in attendance was Governor Fritz Hollings.

I was required to go on a midshipman cruise the summer after graduating from USC in May of 1958. The cruise was out of Long Beach, California where my mother's brother, Rossa Cox, lived. He was a retired United States Naval Warrant officer who lived with his wife, Rose, and two sons Richard and Jackie. I was at port most of the four weeks of the cruise, being on alert to deploy to the Mediterranean Lebanese Crisis. I got to spend some time with Rossa and his family and to see some of the area. After the cruise, I was promoted to Ensign and received orders to the *USS Rhodes DER 384*, home ported in Newport, Rhode Island.

Peggy and I were married on August 16, 1958 at the Prince George Winyah Episcopal Church in Georgetown, South Carolina. I was married wearing my Naval dress whites with my father as my best man. Peggy was a beautiful bride wearing a gorgeous gown provided for her by a dear friend MaryBelle Dunn. The reception was held at the Georgetown Country Club for about 100 guests. We went to Charleston, South Carolina the next day for a two-day honeymoon, just prior to departing for Newport, Rhode Island. I had a reporting date of August 23, 1958.

Stacy and Peggy's Wedding,
1958

CHAPTER FIVE
USS RHODES DER-384
Newport, Rhode Island
1958-1960

Peggy and I de-
parted, along with
her Boston Ter-
rier dog, Toby, for
Newport, Rhode
Island on August
20, 1958. We
took off in style
with the 1951
Ford, given to me
by my Daddy
during my sophomore year at the University of South
Carolina. The trunk and the back seat were full of clothes
and wedding presents. Toby and our black and white 13"
television rode at the top of the pile.

Peggy by the 1951 Ford

We traveled Highway 17 to Norfolk, Virginia, then took
the Chesapeake Bay ferry to Highway 13 to Wilmington,
Delaware. From there, we traveled to the New Jersey
Turnpike and on to the George Washington Parkway.
When we got to the George Washington Bridge, there was
a sign saying "Exact Change" lane, which I was in. I did
not have the required change at the time, so I stopped.
People in line behind me blew their horns and screamed
at me so vehemently, that I departed and ran the toll. On
my way from there to Newport, I kept glancing in the rear
view mirror waiting for a cop to stop me but that never
happened. I got away with it!

Peggy with Boston terrier, Toby, at 16 Everett Street, 1959

When we arrived in Newport, we found a boarding house that was very near the old Viking Hotel. A Mrs. Mickle owned it, and she was kind enough to take us to one of her rental homes the next day. We decided to rent a first floor, one bedroom apartment at 16 Everett Street for $75.00 per month, including the utilities.

I reported to the *Rhodes* on August 23rd as ordered. The only way to get to the ship was via a small ferry that ran to Goat Island where the ship was moored. When I reported aboard, the officer

USS Rhodes DER384

of the deck was First Lieutenant Jim Miller. We got underway on August 25th for a thirty-day DEW (Defense Early Warning) as a picket ship in the North Atlantic. The DEW line ran from Argentina, to Newfoundland, to the Azores which was about one thousand miles. There were four stations that were two hundred and fifty miles apart. We spent a few days on each station. At the end of the fourth station, we would return thirty days later to Newport.

The seas picked up immediately departing Newport. I became sea sick within the first hour of our departure. I was sea sick for five days. The first two days I thought that I was going to die. The last three days, I was afraid that I was not going to die. The second class gunner's mate, who was standing watch on the bridge, probably saved my life. He provided me with a block of cheese for one pocket and saltine crackers for the other one. He instructed me to take a bite of each after every sickness and sure enough it eventually worked.

The wardroom officers during my tour were Commanding Officer, Lieutenant Commander Petroff, then Lieutenant Commander Cannon and, later on, Lieutenant Commander Kleist. The Executive Officers were Lieutenant Charlie Mann and Lieutenant Les Etcherson. The Operations Lieutenants were Lieutenant Jim McKinnon and Lieutenant Junior Grade Bill Cox, and the Communications Officer was Lieutenant Junior Grade McKinley. Engineering Officer was Lieutenant Junior Grade Tom Brummit, and Supply Officers were Lieutenant Junior Grade Bruce Avery and Ensign Randy Robertson. The Gunnery Officer was Lieutenant Junior Grade Bob Gardner, and the Electronic Material Officer was Ensign Adams. The First Lieutenant was Ensign Jim Miller.

During my tour on the Rhodes, I served as Communications Officer, Custodian of Registered Publications, Crypto Officer and later as Combat Information Officer. I made five, thirty-day pickets, and was absent the first two Christmases of our marriage. I made one patrol off Iceland.

All the storms that blew up the east coast came through this area. We experienced sixty-foot seas rolling fifty-five degrees and icy conditions sometimes top side in the winter. We lost the steel gun tub on Mount 51 on the bow, which was about four inches of thick steel, to a big wave that came across the bow and ripped it out, so that we had a hole in the bow on the deck. I lost about 15 pounds during the thirty-day pickets. I thought on a couple of occasions that I was saying my last prayer because the storm got so intense.

My last picket was between Iceland and the Faroe Islands. We visited Greenock, Scotland in the Furth of Clyde. I attended a party with some wardroom officers while at port, where I tasted my first drink of scotch.

I took a train from Liverpool to London, England and then flew back to the United States on a military plane. I arrived in Trenton, New Jersey, then departed to New York City, New York, where I took a train to Providence, Rhode Island, and then a bus to Newport, Rhode Island, so that I could retrieve my 1957 turquoise Chevrolet convertible. Then, I embarked on a twenty hour drive — non-stop — to Georgetown, South Carolina.

My wife, Peggy, was to deliver our son, Stacy III, around the end of the month. Stacy III had other plans and did not arrive until September 10, 1960. My Daddy stayed with me at the hospital throughout the night to make sure that we named the baby Herman Stacy Clardy, III if we had a son. I was in receipt of orders to the District Intelligence Office in Charleston, South Carolina.

CHAPTER SIX
Charleston, South Carolina
1960-1962

I reported for duty in September
at the District Intelligence Office in Charleston, South Carolina. The officer in charge was
Captain Sadler and later Captain
Hankey. The Executive Officer
was Commander McIntosh.
These men were my bosses during my two-year tour in Charleston.

Federal Agent Stacy Clardy, 1960

I was assigned as Administrative Officer for the first few
months, then as a Naval District Intelligence agent. I wore
civilian clothes and carried a badge. I performed background investigations on military personnel and civilians.
Then I started investigating homosexuals, known as
"6J's." I became very efficient in identifying them and
having them administratively discharged.

We spent three weeks each summer at Pawleys Island,
South Carolina at the "Mary Lou" owned by Daddy and
his friend Laurice Rhem. Peggy always took a maid to
take care of our children, Stacy III and Chris, who was
born on December 1, 1961.

After the arduous sea duty, I gained weight, blooming
from 160 pounds to 170 plus, so I decided to cut back on
my intake of food and booze. I took up golf at the course
on the base and became the champion in 1961.

We rented an apartment in a quadraplex with two bedrooms and one bath at 640 Windermere Boulevard in Charleston, South Carolina. It was located near Trinity Episcopal Church where we attended services. I had an old 14-foot wooden boat and an 18-horsepower Johnson outboard motor. It was used to water ski at the Wapoo cut and the Ashley River. I received orders to be Operations Officer on the *USS Roan DD-853* in July of 1962.

CHAPTER SEVEN
USS CHARLES H ROAN DD-853
Newport, Rhode Island
1962-1963

I flew by military plane to Guantanamo Bay, Cuba, better known as "Gitmo," and reported for duty as the Operations Officer. The ship was undergoing refresher training, which consisted of daily operations, one gunnery,

USS Charles R. Roan DD 853, Operations Officer

submarine-warfare and engineering trials, culminating in an operational readiness inspection at the end of training. As Operations Officer, I controlled operations from the combat information center. The ship performed well and passed all phases of the inspection. The following article, written by me, appears in the Jolly Cholly (the Roan's newsletter), about the Cuban crisis:

The ship was in Newport, Rhode Island in early October after completing refresher training in Guantanamo Bay, NGFS qualifications at Culebra, port visit to San Juan and serving as Sonar School Ship at Key West, Florida. President Kennedy had established a blockade of Cuba due to the Russian buildup of missiles that were a threat to the U.S. All ships were ordered to be ready to deploy to Cuba.

The wardroom officers were having a party Saturday to celebrate being home. About 2000 hours, I received a phone call from DESLANT (Destroyer Force Atlantic) operations to get underway A.S.A.P. This really broke up the party! Weekend liberty had been granted with permission of SOPA (Senior Officer Present Afloat). The ship sailed the next day, leaving 34 shipmates on the beach. These men would join the ship during the deployment. The Roan joined the Task Group in route south, which included USS Independence CVA 62, an AO (Fleet Oiler), an AE (Ammunition Ship) and seven Destroyers ready for war.

The wardroom officers included: Commanding Officer, Commander Charles Hayden (deceased); Executive Officer, Lieutenant Commander Larry Treadwell; Operations Officer, Lieutenant Stacy Clardy; Engineering Officer, Lieutenant Bob Comey (deceased); Gunnery, Lieutenant John Chernaud; Supply Officer, Lieutenant Junior Grade Joe Mathias; Combat Information Officer, Lieutenant Junior Grade Gordon Silcox; Communications Officer, Ensign Charlie Wingo; Electronic Material Officer, Ensign Brian Woodward (deceased); Damage Control Assistant, Ensign Bill Effird; and Destroyer Anti-Submarine Helicopter, Lieutenant Junior Grade Larry Thomas.

Operations during deployment included refueling, plane guarding, Anti-Submarine Warfare and acting as Screen Commander. While performing as Screen Commander the outstanding performance by Chief Thomas Hoffman of the radar team and Chief James Quigley Signalman Chief, and Richard Souza Signalman First Class, of the signal gang resulted in a BZ (or "Well done") from the Commodore.

One of my very favorite memories was watching Commander Hayden guiding the Charles H. Roan and her crew through this tense time in history. All ships' personnel received the Navy Expeditionary Medal. Roan completed all commitments in an outstanding manner.

Cuban Missile Crisis, 1962

The ship made a name for itself during an operation with a nuclear submarine Scorpion, an attack submarine. *Roan* fired an ASROC, an anti-submarine rocket, at the submarine during an exercise and actually hit the submarine. The ACO feature, that is an automatic cut-off feature, did not properly function and the torpedo went through the propeller of the submarine and bent it.

The Commanding Officer came on Gertrude, which is an underwater telephone, very upset with the captain. He had to come to the surface and return to port. We followed him into port. Our skipper, driving that old WWII Destroyer, became very famous for taking out a modern attack submarine.

The *Roan* was one of the first ships to fly the DASH (Destroyer Anti-Submarine Helo). We made a port visit to Washington, D.C., rendering honors to Mount Vernon as we passed President Washington's home to visit the Navy Yard in the city. The Chief of Naval Operations visited the ship in the yard to watch the operations.

Peggy and the boys moved to 27 Burdick Avenue, in Newport, Rhode Island, about a mile from the base. This

1963 - NaNa, Bertie, Maude, Suzanna, John, Daphinia, Chris and Stacy III

was a three bedroom house with a finished basement and rented for $100.00 a month. We lived there until 1965. I received orders in November of that year to be Executive Officer of the *USS Hissem DER-400*, also home-ported in Newport.

CHAPTER EIGHT
USS Hissem DER-400
Newport, Rhode Island
1964-1965

The *Hissem* was on a
nine-month deployment
to Antarctica operating
out of Dunedin, New
Zealand. The Command-
ing Officer wanted me to
fly out before Christmas
to make an indoctrination
picket, thirty days prior to
relieving the Executive
Officer. I convinced Commander Patilla, the commander
of the escort squadron, CORTRON 18, not to send me
out until after the first of the year, so the family could be
together for Christmas.

USS Hissem Der 400, Executive Officer

I flew with the squadron's Chaplain, Lieutenant Skip
Vogel, via military aircraft, from Andrews Air Force Base
to Pearl Harbor, Hawaii, to Christ Church, New Zealand
to join the ship at Dunedin. We made one, thirty-day
picket to sixty degrees south prior to departure for home
via Hobart, Tasmania; Adelaide, Australia; Perth,
Australia; Singapore; Bombay (Mumbai), India; Athens,
Greece; Cannes, France; Barcelona, Spain and the
Azores, arriving back in Newport, Rhode Island on the
May 15, 1964.

The ship crossed the equator in route, and the Chaplain
and I had to go through the initiation from Pollywog to
Shellback. This meant that, according to tradition, the

crew who had already been across the equator going to New Zealand put us through garbage shoots, beat us with fire hoses and more or less intimidated us. They had a good time with Chaplain Lieutenant Skip Vogel and me, while Captain Fontaine stayed in his cabin and left our physical well-being and dignity to their discretion.

While we were in Dunedin, the ship's Captain Fontaine taught ship handling. On one occasion, I was getting the ship underway from the pier, and the anchor got hung up under the pier bending the shank. The Commanding Officer took the blame for the incident, but I had a hard time living that one down. The Commanding Officer was an outstanding ship handler and taught me well.

Lieutenant Commander Fontaine was relieved by Lieutenant Commander Dean, a man who was a Staff Officer type with very little ship board experience. Peggy gave a "Hail and Farewell" party for the two of them and served beef stroganoff to all the officers and their wives. It was a great event.

The ship was later assigned to picket duty off Cuba, at Dog Rocks, during one of the missile crises with Cuba. In transit from Newport, Rhode Island to Key West, Florida, we hit a bad storm that was actually the tail end of a hurricane off Cape Hatteras. The new Commanding Officer looked bad and scared.

Upon arrival in Key West, he had the CON (control of the ship) as we approached the pier. I was the navigator and asked him to slow down which he did. As we approached the assigned pier, I asked him again to slow down, and he did. As we got to the place for the landing, he did not do anything, so I gave orders to the helm and made the landing myself. From then on, I gave all of the orders for the approach to the berth.

One time while we were making a visit to Port Everglades, Florida, my mother's sister, Aunt Daisy, and her husband, Johnny, who was a Captain with Eastern Airlines, picked me up and took me to their home. They were living in Coral Gables, Florida at the time. Johnny and I played golf at the Coral Gables Country Club, and he beat me. I received orders in June to be the Naval Exchange Officer to the Royal Canadian Navy at Her Majesty's Station STADACONA, Halifax, Nova Scotia.

Officers serving aboard the *USS Hissem DER 400* were: Commanding Officers Lieutenant Commander Rich Fontaine, Lieutenant Commander Ron Dean; Executive Officers, Lieutenant Bob Durbin, Lieutenant Stacy Clardy; Operations Officer Kip Schmidt; Engineering Officer Howard McKinley; Supply Officer Ken Tholan; Electronic Material Officer Tom Mullaney; Damage Control Assistant Officer Ray Montminney; Main Propulsion Assistant Officer Ted Vaccarilla; Commanding Officer Neal Hayes; Combat Information Officer Wes Moir; First Lieutenant Officer Mike Klyzeiko.

During these two years while serving on the *USS Hissem* in Newport, my sister, Susan, married Doctor Maxwell Ezell Cline. The wedding took place on September 12, 1964 at Duncan Memorial Church in Georgetown. Peggy and I, along with our sons Stacy and Chris, drove to South Carolina for this very special event in our family. Susan made a beautiful bride.

Susan and Ezell later became the parents of two children: my nephew, Max, and my niece, Paige. Paige is currently

married to a nice young man named Kendrick Sternberg. They have a son, Seth, and live in Charlotte, North Carolina. Her brother, Max, lives in Charleston and enjoys the life of a bachelor!

Paige with husband, Kendrick, and son, Seth, in 2010

CHAPTER NINE
HMS Stadacona
Halifax, Nova Scotia
1965-1967

Peggy, Stacy III, Chris and I, along with our beagle, Hunter, drove my new 1964 Impala Chevrolet to Halifax, Nova Scotia from Pawleys Island, South Carolina. We arrived the last week of May and stayed at the Wedgewood Motel for a few days while

Mother, Peggy, Daddy and boys in Halifax, 1966

looking for a home. We finally found one near the hotel at 52 Wedgewood Avenue, which was about four miles from the base. The home had three bedrooms, two fireplaces and one bathroom.

Hunter, my beagle

I reported the last day of May to the Fleet School for duty as an instructor in operations. My job consisted of training officers in ASW (Anti-Submarine Warfare) and fleet maneuvering. My boss was Lieutenant Commander Vern Blair. He liked his beer at noon, and I joined him for a while, but I soon realized I could not drink and be alert to teach in the afternoon!

There was a gymnasium nearby, so I learned to play squash instead of drinking during the noon hour. I also took up curling on the weekends. The family learned to ice skate, toboggan, and the boys played ice hockey on a small rink with the next-door neighbor. The winters were cold: Golf was only played three months of the year.

Being congratulated at Royal Canadian Navy, Halifax, Nova Scotia, 1965-7

During my time with the Royal Canadian Navy, they went through an integration program to roll all their services into one. This was a very sad time for the Royal Canadian Navy, for they had a long and proud tradition similar to the Royal Navy of England.

My son, Stacy, attended a primary grade for five year olds and he walked to school, about five blocks away, with the other kids in the neighborhood. We visited Pawleys Island, South Carolina each summer for a pleasant change of temperature.

The Counselor General provided me with a case of booze each month for about two dollars a bottle. Daddy and Mama visited one time, and Peggy put on a party with great food and drinks. The party celebrated my selection to Lieutenant Commander and was meant to be a two-hour affair. However, the attendees stayed past midnight. They would not leave until all the booze was gone. This was typical of Canadians because they loved their booze.

We made some great friends and enjoyed the tour very much. Other United States exchange officers there during my tour were Lieutenant Ray Hart, who had been a friend of mine throughout the years, and Lieutenant Commander Glen Bates. I did have the opportunity to go to sea in one of their destroyers during my tour of duty for an exercise. They had a bar in the ward room at which I enjoyed myself very much!

In April of 1967, I was selected to attend the Naval War College in Newport, Rhode Island as a student. We departed in May of 1967 for Newport.

CHAPTER TEN
United States Naval War College
Newport, Rhode Island
1967-1968

We found a home at 159 Coggeshall Avenue in the old section of Newport, Rhode Island near the ocean. The boys attended Carey Elementary about five blocks away, and they could walk to school. The course I attended was entitled Command and Staff. It was a ten-month academic year consisting of attending lectures by professors and dignitaries, classes in strategic planning and fleet operations and tactics. We were required to write staff studies and operation orders and prepare a thesis of at least 60 pages.

I had been out of college for nine years and needed to make adjustments back to the academic environment. I took a speed reading course to help with the voluminous amount of reading requirements. I decided to write my thesis entitled "The Canadian Armed Forces: Is it significant to the defense of North America?" I struggled all year and finally got the preliminary paper approved by the staff. Peggy was kind enough to type the rough draft, and I had the final paper professionally done.

While a student in Newport, Rhode Island, we were allowed to play golf at the Newport Country Club, the site of the first U.S. Open in 1894. After class on Friday, the Officers' Club, at a very scenic location on Narragansett Bay, would be host a very raucous happy hour. All the students would gather there for a good old party. I made some great friends during my tour of duty there, one being Lieutenant Commander John Paul Jones. Another was Major Jim Levett who visited me after the course was over down in Pawleys Island, South Carolina, where we played golf at the Dunes Golf Club in Myrtle Beach, South Carolina. I purchased the "Mary Lou" house and an adjacent lot from my Daddy and Mr. Rhem for $12,000.00 in 1967.

I graduated in May and received orders to the *USS Vesole DD-878* as the Executive Officer, home-ported in Newport, Rhode Island.

CHAPTER ELEVEN
USS VESOL DD-878
Newport, Rhode Island and Charleston,'South Carolina
1968-1970

Showing off at the Bahrain Officers'Club, 1970

I reported in June while the ship was in the Boston Naval Shipyard undergoing a six-month overhaul. I relieved Lieutenant Commander John Kristoff and assumed the duties as Executive Officer under Commanding Officer Peter Orvis. He was a micro-manager and difficult to work with in every way. Other officers were: Operations Officer, Lieutenant Kevin Healy; Gunnery Officer, Lieutenant Joe Bishop; Anti-Submarine Warfare Officer, Ensign Gus Gustofferson; Navigator, Lieutenant Paul Mahlstedt; Engineering Officer, Lieutenant Carl; the Main Assistant (MPA), Lieutenant Junior Grade Owen Chapman; Communications Officer, Ensign Nick Acoff; Supply Officer, Lieutenant Don Schwab.

The ship completed overhaul and departed to undergo refresher training at Gitmo. In the first few weeks there, Lieutenant Carl, our Engineering Officer, had a nervous breakdown as a result of all the stress of the job. He reported to the hospital at Gitmo and did not return to our ship. Then the Captain appointed me to be Engineering Officer as well as the Executive Officer.

A Lieutenant Gary Cline had orders to be the chief Engineering Officer on the ship. He was in Destroyers' school in Newport, Rhode Island. I made a call to him and convinced him that it would be in his best interest to report early. He flew down soon after graduation and reported for duty. (Gary and his wife, Sylvia, presently live on Little Oak Island in Folly Beach, South Carolina. We have remained friends to this day.) The ship returned to Newport and underwent local operations for the rest of the year.

Peggy and I had a New Year's Eve party at the house for all the officers and their wives. The celebrating went on very late. I received a phone call about six o'clock the following morning from Kathleen Dudley, my mother-in-law, that my Daddy had died at the

Kathleen Dudley with Mother, Barbara, Kathleen, Susan Cline, Alisha

Georgetown Memorial Hospital of a heart attack. We packed up and drove to Georgetown, South Carolina to attend the funeral. The ship was scheduled to change home ports to Charleston, South Carolina during this period of time, so I left the family in Georgetown. The boys attended school in Georgetown for about six months.

Then during the deployment, Peggy found a place to live on Parish Road in Charleston, and the boys were able to attend St. Andrews school nearby. Our deployment was with the standing NATO Naval Force Atlantic. This was a Force made up of ships from England, the Netherlands, Norway, Italy and Turkey. In December, the Force visited Den Helder, Netherlands. Peggy and some of the officers' wives flew over for a Christmas visit, and we

The Netherlands, Christmas, 1970

took leave and visited Amsterdam, Paris, Ant-werp, and Luxembourg.

The ship also visited Izmir, Turkey; Trondheim and Bergen, Norway; Naples and Taranto, Italy; the Madeira Islands and London, England. While in London, Princess Margaret hosted a cocktail party aboard one of the English ships for the officers. She was a very petite lady with a big smile. She greeted each officer and drank with a silver stirrer in her glass.

I experienced a serious confrontation with Commanding Officer Peter Orvis over a fitness report that he wrote about me. It would have ended my naval career. He backed down after our discussion and wrote another report stating that the previous one was a mistake. He was relieved by Commander Stephen Hart, a very fine man and a pleasant change!

The ship deployed from Charleston, South Carolina to the Middle East for six months in January of 1970 visiting Monrovia, Liberia; Luanda, Angola; Lourenco Marques, Mozambique; Mombasa, Kenya; Djibouti and the Maltese and Colombo Ceylon (Sri Lanka), as it was called then. The ship also visited the beautiful Maldives Islands that are surrounded by coral reefs. The ambassador to Ceylon, the Honorable Robert Strausz-Hupe, visited the ship in order to present his credentials.

I was relieved in Colombo and received orders to become the Chief Staff Officer to Destroyer Squadron 24 back in

Newport, Rhode Island. After being relieved, I returned via TWA on what was called an "around the world flight," first to New York City and then down to Charleston, South Carolina.

CHAPTER TWELVE
Destroyer Squadron 24
Newport, Rhode Island
1970-1971

The family and I spent about four weeks in Pawleys Island, South Carolina prior to departure back to Newport, Rhode Island. I bought a new gray 1970 Chevrolet Impala convertible that I still own to this day to replace my 1964. I towed Daddy's old 1970 Chevrolet to be our second car.

Clardy Family, 1970

We found government housing at 196 Jones Street, Middletown, Rhode Island, about two blocks from the base. It was a three-bedroom home with one bathroom and a carport. Our neighbors included Lieutenant Commander Ron Forst and his family, and they have remained close friends to this day. My bosses were Captain Kiley and later Captain Johnson. I relieved Lieutenant Commander McGanka as Chief Staff Officer. Other officers on the staff were: Lieutenant Kristensen, Lieutenant Serry and Lieutenant Junior Grade Meyer. The staff went to sea one time during my tour for about ten days for an anti-submarine warfare operation to evaluate the difference between the SQS-24 sonar versus the new SQS-26 sonar.

During the American Cup races in 1970 between *Intrepid* and *Gretel Two*, we were embarked in the *Joseph P. Kennedy DD-850*. We hosted Mrs. Jackie Kennedy, her children Caroline and John, her guest, Pearl Mester, and also Secret Service detail for a day of racing. I had lunch with her and her guest along with Commodore Kiley and Commanding Officer Captain Rodgers in the ward room. Jackie was not very talkative, but Pearl carried the conversation and validated her title as "Hostess with the Most-ess."

I played golf at Newport Country Club and squash with Captain Kiley and tennis with Captain Johnson. I received orders to Washington, D.C. to the Naval Material Command, which at that time was commanded by Admiral Ike Kidd. That Commander Rich Fontaine was his Executive Assistant is probably the reason that I received orders to that command.

CHAPTER THIRTEEN
Naval Material Command
Washington, D.C.
1971-1974

After scouring Virginia and Maryland, we found a place to live with the help of an old friend Bruce Avery who served as Supply Officer on the Rhodes. He was the aide to the Vice-Commander in the Naval Material Command where I was reporting. We found a corner condo with four bedrooms and two and one-half baths at 10417 Kardwright Court, Montgomery Village, in Gaithersburg, Maryland. The condo was about thirty-one miles to my office in Crystal City. I bought a new 1972 Vega, silver with a black racing stripe, to replace Dad's old 1970 that broke down.

My position at the Command was Executive Assistant to the Deputy Chief of Naval Material for Administration and Personnel located on the ninth floor of the Crystal City Five. I worked for Captain McClure first and then Captain Murtha as their assistant.

The boys attended the Montgomery county schools in the Montgomery Village. It was a superb school system. They played football and participated in Boy Scouts. My job was mostly doing paperwork, briefing senior officers and attending meetings — not my cup of tea. I did play a good bit of golf with Rich Fontaine on various courses at Quantico and Fort Belvoire. I joined Montgomery Village Country Club in the community where I lived, which is a very good golf course. The commute to work got old very quickly.

The best part of the tour was being selected for Commander. I was also selected to command destroyers. I received orders to be Commanding Officer on the *USS Mullinnix DD-944*.

CHAPTER FOURTEEN
USS Mullinnix DD-944
Norfolk, Virginia
1974-1976

The family moved to Virginia Beach, Virginia and found a new five-bedroom home with three baths at 18 Timberlake Drive in the Kempsville area of Virginia Beach. Stacy and Chris attended Kempsville High School, which was part of an excellent school system. They also continued with Boys Scouts. I bought a 16-foot, fiberglass Galaxy boat and a 70-horsepower motor for skiing and fishing. My mother-in-law, wife, son and I fished the Virginia Capes bridge and tunnel area and caught some large bluefish. We also fished in the Chesapeake Bay, as well as skied in the Intercostal Waterway and at the creek at Pawleys. I have since taught a great number of kids to waterski.

My hair began to thin, so I had a hair transplant in Bethesda, Maryland. Dr. Cameron performed the surgery, and Mama and Aunt Daisy paid for it. Mama wanted me to stay young!

I was assigned duty on the staff of Commander Cruiser Destroyer Force Atlantic for about six months prior to joining the ship. I worked and reported to Commander Destroyer Squadron Two who was Captain Snodgrass and later Captain Kennebrew. The ship was on a six-month deployment to the Middle East.

In April of 1974, I flew on commercial air via Lisbon, Portugal to Lourenco Marques, Mozambique with Lieutenant Bill Triplett, who was later to become my Supply Officer, to meet the *Mullinnix*. I sailed on the ship from Mozambique to Mombasa, Kenya and relieved the Commanding Officer on April 10, 1974.

The *Mullinnix* was a 418-foot Forest Sherman class destroyer weighing 3,400 tons. It had three, five-inch 54 guns and one, three-inch 50 dual gun, MK 32 torpedoes with a 70,000 shaft horsepower. It had four big boilers and four main engines, two big propellers and two big rudders. It was considered the Cadillac of destroyers at that time.

USS Mullinnix DD-944

The ship visited Djibouti, Muscat Oman, Banda Abbas, Iran, Kuwait, Bahrain, Port Louis, Mauritius. Then it went by way of the Cape of Good Hope to Luanda, Angola; Recife, Brazil; San Juan, Puerto Rico and then back to Norfolk, Virginia. We arrived on August 30, 1974.

Officers of the ward room were: Executive Officers Lieutenant Commander Mezmalis, Lieutenant Commander Joe Saul, Lieutenant Commander Larry Bissonnette; Operations Officer Mike Chamberlain; Gunnery Officer, Lieutenant Mike Born; Engineering Officers, Lieutenant Willie Sweat and Lieutenant Commander Bruce Brown; Supply Officer Lieutenant Bill Triplett; Anti-Submarine Warfare, Lieutenant Junior Grade Sanka Blanton; Damage Control, Assistant Lieutenant Junior Grade Tom Schmucker; Ensign Bruce Spalding; Electronic Material Officer, Chief Warrant Officer Eubanks; Main Propulsion System, Ensign Morton; Communications, Ensign Tom Leverage; Navigator, Lieutenant LaMartin; the Chief of the ship was Master Chief Carl Ross.

During the deployment to the Middle East, the *Mullinnix* towed the French *Frigate Balney*, which had lost power for two days in the Gulf of Aiden. We received a "well done" from Commander of the Middle East Force for that operation.

During Caribex, which was a Caribbean exercise in 1975, the *Mullinnix* embarked Vice-Admiral Shennanhan, Commander of the 2nd Fleet for about ten days of an exercise because his flag ship — a cruiser — could not get underway.

In October of 1975, the *Mullinnix* steamed to Gibraltar for a deployment to the Mediterranean to join the NATO On-Call Force in Izmir, Turkey. The Force consisted of: a Turkish Commodore, a Turkish ship, a British ship and an Italian ship. The Force steamed for about thirty days, visiting Cagliari, Sardinia; Taranto and Naples, Italy; and Antalya, Turkey. The last ports of call were Siracusa and Taormina, Sicily and Toulon, France.

Commanding Officer, 1974-6

I was relieved in Genoa, Italy on March 24, 1976 by Commander Tom Anderson. I had a great time in command and made two major deployments with no significant engineering problems. Peggy joined me in Naples, Italy for Christmas in 1975, and we had a joyous time visiting Rome and the Isle of Capri. I then received orders to be the Commanding Officer of the Recruiting District in San Antonio, Texas.

CHAPTER FIFTEEN
Navy Recruiting District
San Antonio, Texas
1976-1979

San Antonio, Texas, 1976, with Bob Hope

I relieved the Commanding Officer of the Navy Recruiting District (NRD), Commander Tex Triber, at the Alamo in July of 1976. Mama, Aunt Daisy and family attended the Change of Command. The area of the Command covered 78,000 square miles from Brownsville in the south, to Del Rio in the west, to Victoria in the east and to St. Angelo in the north.

I had eighty enlisted recruiters and twenty-one recruiting offices throughout the area. My Executive Officers were Lieutenant. Commander Joe Howell and Lieutenant Commander Gary Calnan and four other officers responsible for recruiting and enlisting officers into the United States Navy. Our job was to make the monthly goal assigned by the Recruiting Command in Washington, D.C.

The family settled into a new four-bedroom, two and one-half bath home at 13620 Carlton Oaks, just north of the airport and about four miles from my headquarters in a shopping complex at 102 West Rector. The people of San Antonio were very friendly, and, since this was typically an Air Force and Army town, they thought the Navy was something extra special! The Mayor actually had a Navy background. The city put on river parades and night parades down the streets called Festival San Antonio.

Peggy became sick in late October of 1977 with liver disease. I sent her home, hoping that Mama and Dr. Varn could make her well. She died at the Georgetown Memorial Hospital on December 12, 1977. She is buried in the family plot in Andrews, South Carolina. After Peggy died, the boys and I kept it together the best we could by cooking our meals each night and doing house chores. Stacy III made Eagle Scout, and Chris made Life Scout in 1978. Also, they both had paper routes in the neighborhood where we lived. I gave Stacy III my 1972 Vega and bought Chris a 1967 Galaxie 500 Ford.

Stacy and Jeanne's Wedding, 1979

I met Jeanne Cress Mason, who had previously worked in Washington, D.C. for Chief Justice Renquist and Richard Nixon's re-election committee before moving to San Antonio to be with her mother, Lucelle Cress. While there, she had entered the Catholic Convent, but decided against becoming a nun. She then worked in an art gallery in the same building as my headquarters. We dated and later married on January 29, 1979 in D'hanis, Texas by Father Tony Costantino. We took our honeymoon in Acapulco, Mexico. (Jeanne has two brothers: Bill, who is married to Fran, with two daughters Amanda and Dawn; and retired USMC Master Sergent Jim Cress, who is married to Vicki, with one daughter, Kim.)

Since I traveled often, I bought skis and went skiing at Copper Mountain outside of Denver, Colorado every time we had a meeting in Denver. My area Commanders were Captain Burnett and later Captain Hagburg with headquarters in Dallas,

Honeymoon, 1979

Texas. The area command consisted of Naval Recruiting District (NRD)-Denver, NRD-Houston, NRD-New Orleans, NRD-Dallas, NRD-Albuquerque and NRD-Oklahoma City. The Commanding Officer for Oklahoma was Commander Mannie Hendrix, an outstanding Naval Aviator, who has remained my friend for the past 36 years.

Stacy III's graduation, 1978

Stacy III graduated Churchill High School in 1978 and enrolled at the University of Texas in Austin, where he joined the ROTC program. He later received a full Naval ROTC scholarship to the University of South Carolina. Chris graduated in 1979 and attended USC for one year before joining the United States Navy. Their best friends in San Antonio were Darren and Greg Hickman who lived in the same neighborhood and went to the same high school. I played golf at Fort Sam Houston Army base and several public courses.

Chris' graduation, 1979

Change of Command, St. Anthony Hotel, 1979

I sold the home at Carlton Oaks Avenue and moved to Sun Trail, which was about a mile away from our previous home and lived there for the remainder of the tour. The change of command was held at St. Anthony's Hotel in March of 1979, and Commander Leslie Sanders relieved me there. I received orders back to Washington, D.C. to the Naval Material Command.

CHAPTER SIXTEEN
Naval Material Command
Washington, D.C.
1979-1982

The family spent three weeks at the Mary Lou house at Pawleys Island, South Carolina prior to departure to Washington which turned out to be my last tour of duty. While at the beach, I received a phone call from my good friend Commander Ron Forst in Washington, D.C. telling me that my name was on the list for promotion to Captain. Mama was with us during this time at the beach, and we had a great old party.

I reported to the Chief of Naval Material in July. I was spot-promoted to Captain without an increase in pay for the first year. My title was Assistant Deputy Chief of Naval Material for Munitions and Physical Security for the United States Navy. This included nuclear weapons, worldwide security of sensitive conventional arms, ammunitions and explosives.

Washington, D.C., 1980

We stayed with Jeanne's friends Helene and Jim Markham and their son, Michael, while looking for a home. They lived in one of Paul Mellon's homes on Whitehaven Street off Constitution Avenue behind the British Embassy. We found a one bedroom, one and one-half bath condo at a place called Watergate-at-Landmark.

The complex had four, 18-story buildings and a squash court with a running track. I had gotten into running in San Antonio before I departed. While in Washington, I ran the Herndon Ten-Miler and the Annapolis, Maryland One-Half Marathon in preparation for the Marine Corp Marathon on November 1, 1981. Unfortunately, I hit the wall at 23 miles and finished the race in four and one-half hours.

We spent every vacation at Pawleys Island, South Carolina and decided to build a beach house in October of 1981. We finished it in March of 1982 and dubbed it the "Captain's Cabin." It is where we still live today. The cost: $80,000. Jeanne stayed at Kathleen's beach house across the street and supervised the construction with Chris's help. Stacy III was attending USC, and Chris was in the Navy serving in the nuclear submarines as an electronic technician. I retired February 1, 1982 after twenty- nine years of service to the United States Navy.

CHAPTER SEVENTEEN
Pawleys Island, South Carolina
1982-2011

In 1982, I attended Real Estate School and obtained my real estate license. I worked from 1982-1998 for the James W. Smith Real Estate Company. The owner, Jimmy Smith, was from a family in Andrews that was close friends with my parents. Then, from 1998-2002, I was at Pawleys Island Realty. Since 2002, I have been with the Weichert Real Estate Company. I sold beach houses and condos and made some big money during this period of time. I also placed the "Mary Lou" in the rental program with the Pawleys Island Realty Company in 1982 for additional income.

I was fortunate to have Mama living close by in George-town, South Carolina. Her sister, Daisy, moved to Georgetown from Florida in 1974. She eventually moved in with Mama in 1982.

In 1982, I was appointed to the Board of Directors of Pawleys Island Civic Association. In 1985, I served as Chairman of the Incorporation Commission and made Pawleys Island a town. In 1987, I ran for mayor and lost by one vote. The count was Jim Prince with forty-four votes, I with forty-three votes and Luke Ellerbe with thirty-three votes. I also ran for Town Council, but was beaten by ten votes. I initiated the effort that became state law to cap the county property taxes.

Jeanne and I took a trip via C5A military transport plane to Germany and a train down to Paris to see the Dufours. They were friends I met during my stint as Commanding Officer of the *USS Mullinnix*. We also got to fly down to see a friend of mine, Sarah Katarivas, that I had met while in Sicily, Italy. Then we visited Jeanne's mother in San Antonio, Texas. While there, I flew to Denver, Colorado to join Tracy and Alison Forst, along with Stacy and Chris for a skiing trip at Vail for three days. Jeanne and I went on vacations to Bermuda in 1983 and 1999. I played one of the best golf courses in the world, Mid Ocean, while there.

The Fontaines invited Jeanne and me on a golfing trip to Scotland in 1991 for thirty days. We played Royal Troon, Preswick, Old Course at St. Andrews, Lady Bank, Royal Aberdeen, Rosemont, Blairgowrie, Royal Dornict. We toured Edinburgh, Scotland and London, England.

Lancer

Thad

I lost my dog, Lancer, a salt and pepper Schnauzer, when he was 15 years old. So we bought a male Boykin Spaniel and named him Thaddeus or Thad. He ran with me every day for 13 years, then he died. I now have a mixed breed Lab named Lossie that was found by Beth Altman, who talked me into taking her. She chewed and devoured my grandmother NaNa's old furniture on the porch. I was extremely mad, but she has finally become a good dog.

Lossie

Hurricane Hugo struck in 1989 and destroyed the "Mary Lou" totally. The only thing salvaged was the front door of the house. We built another four-bedroom, two bath rental house and named it the "Mary Lou II." Sometime after that, feral cats took up residence in the wooded area next to the "Mary Lou II," and, before we knew it, there were at least ten of them. I started to have the female cats spade, and we carried some of them out to a farm with the help of Nate Portia. He worked for the mayor of Pawleys Island and kept the town clean and well maintained. Coco, Ivan and Flea were three of the feral cats who let you touch them, and so we adopted them into our home.

In 1998, Hurricane Bonnie hit, but she proved to be a minor storm. We evacuated to Mama's house in Georgetown, South Carolina as we did for all hurricanes. I decided to come back and feed the feral cats, but I was stopped at a road block on the south causeway and informed that I could not go back to my house. I ran the road block anyway and the chief of police and several deputies came to my house while I was feeding the cats, handcuffed me and took me to jail, where I spent one night. It was written up in the local paper, and I became an instant hero for all cat lovers in the community.

Aunt Daisy died in 1991 at home, and we buried her in Vero Beach, Florida, alongside her husband, Johnny, who died in 1972. We lost Jeanne's mother in 1992, and she is buried in the National Cemetery beside her husband Lieutenant Colonel Cress in San Antonio, Texas.

Mother had a stroke in 1995 and was in her bed for two and a half years. Susan, my sister, moved from Charleston to be with her, and we had nurses around the clock for those years. She died December 2, 1997 and is buried in our family plot in Andrews, South Carolina. My father's only sister, Bertie Maude, is 97 years young and the only living sibling left of either of my parents. During the past thirty-five years, Bertie married Lieutenant Colonel Bill Peace, who is buried in Andrews Cemetary, and

Stacy and Susan in 2006

George Scraggs, who is buried at All Saints Church, Pawleys Island. Susan now lives in our mother's home and Ezell, Susan's estranged husband, died in 2010.

In late 2001, I separated from my wife Jeanne and moved to the "Treehouse" and then to the "Mary Lou II," while I built an apartment named "Sea Cabin" over the front porch of our beach home, the "Captain's Cabin." I moved into the cabin in 2002. Jeanne moved out in 2003 into a condo that I bought for her at Chapel Creek. We officially divorced in July of 2003.

Stacy and Tracy Clardy, 2005

I started dating again and became seriously involved with a lovely lady, Tracy Gay, from Pawleys Island, South Carolina, whom I later married in August of 2005. We soon parted ways with the marriage legally lasting only a little over two years. We have since made peace with one another. I remarried Jeanne a few months after my divorce from Tracy.

I joined Pawleys Plantation Country Club when it was first developed in 1988. I usually play golf about two times a week. My sons have played golf with me at Pawleys Plantation and other courses in the area many times, but that have never managed to beat me.

I continue to work out every day, jogging, doing sit-ups and push-ups, along with using an abdominal slide. The total distance I have jogged since retirement twenty-nine years ago is about 20,000 miles.

After I retired, I joined All Saints Episcopal Church. Then Jeanne, being Catholic, and I decided we wanted to attend the same church, so we joined Pawleys Island Baptist Church, now known as PICC. We were baptized in the creek together on the south end of the beach on Pawleys Island by the Reverend Bob Barrows.

Stacy and Jeanne Clardy

At the church, we took a course called Navigator 2:7 that was taught by Helen and George Hilliard, and I finally understood the importance of having a personal born-again relationship with Jesus Christ. In 2009, Jeanne and I joined Precious Blood Catholic Church.

I have memorized the following Bible verses from the King James Version and have recited them at night during my prayer time since 1991. They are as follows:

Assurance of Salvation ~ 1 John 5:11-12
"And this is the testimony that God gave us eternal life, and this life is in His Son. He who has the Son has life; he who has not the Son has not life."

Assurance of Answered Prayer ~ John 16:24
"Hitherto you have asked nothing in My Name; ask, and

you will receive, that your joy may be full."

Assurance of Victory ~1 Corinthians 10:13
"No temptation has overtaken you that is not common to man. God is faithful, and He will not let you be tempted beyond your strength, but will also provide the way of escape, that you may be able to endure it."

Assurance of Forgiveness ~ 1 John 1:9
"If we confess our sins, He is faithful and just, and will forgive our sins and cleanse us from unrighteousness."

Assurance of Guidance ~ Proverbs 3:5-6
"Trust in the Lord with all your heart, and do not rely on your own insight. In all your ways acknowledge Him, and He will make straight your paths."

Christ the Center ~ Galatians 2:20
"I have been crucified with Christ, thus it is no longer I who live, but Christ who lives in me; and the life I now live in the flesh, I live by faith in the Son of God who loved me and gave Himself for me."

II Corinthians 5:17
"Therefore, if anyone is in Christ, he is a new creation; the old has passed away, behold, the new has come."

Obedience to Christ ~ John 14:21
"He who has My commandments and keeps them, he it is who loves Me; and he who loves Me will be loved by My Father, and I will love him and manifest myself to him."

Romans 12:1
"I appeal to you therefore, brethren, by the mercies of God, to present your bodies as a living sacrifice, holy and

acceptable to God, which is your spiritual worship."

The Word ~ Joshua 1:8
"Do not let this Book of the Law depart from your mouth; meditate on it day and night, so that you may be careful to do everything written in it. Then you will be prosperous and successful."

II Timothy 3:16
"All Scripture is God-breathed and is useful for teaching, rebuking, correcting and training in righteousness."

Fellowship ~ Hebrews 10:24-25
"And let us consider how we may spur one another on toward love and good deeds. Let us not give up meeting together, as some are in the habit of doing, but let us encourage one another — and all the more as you see the Day approaching."

1 John 1:3
"We proclaim to you what we have seen and heard, so that you also may have fellowship with us. And our fellowship is with the Father and with His Son, Jesus Christ."

Prayer ~ Philippians 4:6-7
"Be anxious for nothing, but in everything by prayer and supplication with thanksgiving let your requests be made known to God. And the peace of God, which surpasses all comprehension, shall guard your hearts and your minds in Christ Jesus."

John 15:7
"If you abide in me, and my words abide in you, ask whatever you will, and it shall be done unto you."

Witnessing ~ Romans 1:16
"I am not ashamed of the gospel, because it is the power of God for the salvation of everyone who believes; first the Jew, then the Gentile."

Matthew 4:19
"Come, follow me," Jesus said, "and I will make you fishers of men."

The view off my front porch is the best at Pawleys Island and will rest your body and soul during quiet time.

Since retirement from the Navy, I have allowed my sons to have one-third ownership of Mary Lou II for an investment of $20,000 each. I have also been Commander of VFW Post 11439, Pawleys Island, South Carolina and served as President of Sertoma.

Stacy III and Chris,
1983 at USC graduation

My sons, Stacy III and Chris have done quite well for themselves. I am very proud of each one!

Stacy III and Barbara's Wedding, 1983

Stacy III graduated from USC in 1983. I swore him in as a 2nd Lieu-tenant in the United States Marine Corp at USC. He married Barbara Stone in 1983 at All Saints Episcopal Church in Pawleys

Stacy III and Kathleen,

68

Island. They have a daughter, Kathleen. She is named for her Grandmother Peggy's mother. Kathleen is 25 at this time of writing my memoirs.

Stacy and Barbara were later divorced, and he is now married to Alison M. Anderson. They have two

Stacy III, Alison, Kathleen, Mary, Shelby

Stacy III and Alison's wedding, 1994

daughters: 14 year-old Mary Lloyd, named for my mother, and 12 year-old Shelby Margaret, named for Alison's mother, Shelby, and her Grandmother Peggy, my first wife.

Stacy has been very successful in the Marine Corp. He commanded a battalion in combat in Iraq and won the Bronze Star with valor. He has also been a regimental commander in Iraq and won the Legion of Merit with valor. This is the subject of another book by me. He is presently Brigadier General in command at Twenty Nine Palms, California.

Stacy III as Grand Marshall of 4th of July Parade, Pawleys

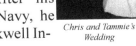

Chris spent six years in the United States Navy and was an E-6 electronics technician in nuclear submarines making 74 day patrols. After his service in the Navy, he worked for Rockwell In-

Chris and Tammie's Wedding

Chris' graduation, CAL State

69

ternational in California. He went to night school at Cal-State Fullerton receiving a double E degree. Then he worked with Lockheed Martin, Boeing Aircraft, and Actel Corporation, before becoming the vice president of Aeroflex Corporation. He is their marketing and sales vice president.

Chris and Jill's Wedding, 2004

Chris married Tammy Jones of Murrells Inlet, South Carolina and is the proud father of a 18 year-old son, Joshua, and 12 year-old daughter, Marissa. He and Tammy later divorced, and he is now married to Jill Tugman who has a 19 year-old son, Tyler. Together Chris and Jill have a son, Joseph Lee (Joe), who turned 5 this summer in July of 2011.

Joshua, Tyler, Marissa and Joe

The Lord has given me good health over the years. I have kept an exercise routine eating proper foods and maintaining my weight. I also think my good health is due to taking Colloidal Life Minerals, fish oil, vitamins B, C and D, CoQ10 Ubiquinol, milk thistle and a baby aspirin daily. I went on blood pressure medicine at age 60 and Zocour for high cholesterol at age 65 to maintain proper levels. For the last two years I have used Jack LaLanne's juicer each day, juicing red grapes, carrots, apples and strawberries.

On October 22, 2011, I won the 5K race at the 20th Annual Pawleys Island Turtle Strut for my age group.

This book is an attempt to fill in the dash on my tombstone. In looking back over my life, I believe the most

Island. They have a daughter, Kathleen. She is named for her Grandmother Peggy's mother. Kathleen is 25 at this time of writing my memoirs.

Stacy and Barbara were later divorced, and he is now married to Alison M. Anderson. They have two

Stacy III, Alison, Kathleen, Mary, Shelby

Stacy III and Alison's wedding, 1994

daughters: 14 year-old Mary Lloyd, named for my mother, and 12 year-old Shelby Margaret, named for Alison's mother, Shelby, and her Grandmother Peggy, my first wife.

Stacy has been very successful in the Marine Corp. He commanded a battalion in combat in Iraq and won the Bronze Star with valor. He has also been a regimental commander in Iraq and won the Legion of Merit with valor. This is the subject of another book by me. He is presently Brigadier General in command at Twenty Nine Palms, California.

Stacy III as Grand Marshall of 4th of July Parade, Pawleys

Chris spent six years in the United States Navy and was an E-6 electronics technician in nuclear submarines making 74 day patrols. After his service in the Navy, he worked for Rockwell In-

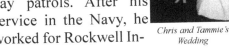

Chris and Tammie's Wedding

Chris' graduation, CAL State

ternational in California. He went to night school at Cal-State Fullerton receiving a double E degree. Then he worked with Lockheed Martin, Boeing Aircraft, and Actel Corporation, before becoming the vice president of Aeroflex Corporation. He is their marketing and sales vice president.

Chris married Tammy Jones of Murrells Inlet, South Carolina and is the proud father of a 18 year-old son, Joshua, and 12 year-old daughter, Marissa. He and Tammy later divorced, and he is now married to Jill Tugman who has a 19 year-old son, Tyler. Together Chris and Jill have a son, Joseph Lee (Joe), who turned 5 this summer in July of 2011.

Chris and Jill's Wedding, 2004

Joshua, Tyler, Marissa and Joe

The Lord has given me good health over the years. I have kept an exercise routine eating proper foods and maintaining my weight. I also think my good health is due to taking Colloidal Life Minerals, fish oil, vitamins B, C and D, CoQ10 Ubiquinol, milk thistle and a baby aspirin daily. I went on blood pressure medicine at age 60 and Zocour for high cholesterol at age 65 to maintain proper levels. For the last two years I have used Jack LaLanne's juicer each day, juicing red grapes, carrots, apples and strawberries.

On October 22, 2011, I won the 5K race at the 20th Annual Pawleys Island Turtle Strut for my age group.

This book is an attempt to fill in the dash on my tombstone. In looking back over my life, I believe the most important thing toward which we should strive is to live by the Fruit of the Spirit. May all who read this be blessed!

Lightning Source UK Ltd.
Milton Keynes UK
UKHW012022040821
388278UK00006B/428/J